Madison County
New York

SOLDIERS

in the
War of 1812

William H. Tuttle

HERITAGE BOOKS
2012

HERITAGE BOOKS
AN IMPRINT OF HERITAGE BOOKS, INC.

Books, CDs, and more—Worldwide

For our listing of thousands of titles see our website at
www.HeritageBooks.com

Published 2012 by
HERITAGE BOOKS, INC.
Publishing Division
100 Railroad Ave. #104
Westminster, Maryland 21157

Originally published by Pipe Creek Publication's
Early Settler Series: New York, No.6
1994

All rights reserved. No part of this book may be reproduced or transmitted in any form or by any means, electronic or mechanical, including photocopying, recording or by any information storage and retrieval system without written permission from the author, except for the inclusion of brief quotations in a review.

International Standard Book Numbers
Paperbound: 978-1-58549-839-0
Clothbound: 978-0-7884-9349-2

PREFACE

The late William Tuttle, one time Madison County Historian compiled a file of those Madison County veterans of the War of 1812 from various sources: pensions, claims against the State for clothing/equipment, etc. for which the individual soldier paid out of pocket; local sources such as cemetery inscriptions, newspaper items et al. The following list is taken from his file, now in the County Historian's office in the Madison County Courthouse in Wampsville, NY.

Madison County researchers owe much to Mr. Tuttle for his never ending quest for local records and for recording those records. I was priveleged to know Mr. Tuttle and to know something of his wide ranging quest. He traveled the county roads looking for abandoned cemeteries - many of which he copied; he haunted the courthouse, he visited libraries throughout the state. He also talked with many of the "old" people he met in his travels and he used some of the tales that were told. There was probably no person who knew as much about the local history; the folklore and folktales of the county as Mr. Tuttle.

Unfortunately he never published the records he accumulated and much of it "drifted away" at his death. In fact at his death, I had the only copy of his monumetal work on the town of Lincoln in my possession. But now with the help of friends, there are four copies in existence - including the original which was returned to the County Historian's office.

We must admire Mr. Tuttle and his lifetime devotion to local history and genealogy under the utmost difficulties. We must bear in mind that at the time Mr. Tuttle was working, there were no xerographic copying machines; typewriters had not yet been electrified; microfilm was not in common usage and computers were as yet undreamed of.

In this copy of Mr. Tuttle's work, we have noted some obvious errors. We advise the reader to check the facts in other sources: cemetery transcriptions, census records, newspaper items or such.

Standard abbreviations are used throughout this work. Names of all locations unless otherwise noted, are those of towns, villages or settlements in Madison County, NY. The Editor will gladlly furnish information to any reader who may be unable to locate a given village or settlement.

At the end of this work, the reader will find a short but most useful bibliography of Madison County, New York sources.

                  Mary K. Meyer, FNGS; FAAGS
                        Editor

MADISON COUNTY, NEW YORK WAR OF 1812 VETERANS

Abbott, John P. — Res.: Hamilton. Claim #9803: $100.00

Ackley, Oliver — Res.: Hamilton. Comm. Officer in the 65th Regt.

Adams, Chapman — Res.: Cazenovia. Claim #3260: $110.00 & Claim #4370: $18.75.

Adams, Frederick M. — Res: Sullivan; 74th Regt.; Capt. in Militia in 1816. Wife, Persis.

Adle, Henry — Res.: Lincoln. 74th Regt.; d. 1822; wife, Catherine.

Aldrich, Uriah — Res: Cazenovia; served with the 8th Cavalry. b. 1782 - d. 1856.

Allen, Caleb, Jr. — Res.: Lenox. Cornet in 74th Regt.; d. 1820

Allen, Daniel — d. 4 Sept. 1876 aged 82 yrs., bur. Merrillsville; owned 50 acre farm in Lenox.

Allen, Ira — Res.: Eaton. Juror in DeRuyter 1808 and in Georgetown in 1815. Daughter, Catherine d. Morrisville 15 Sept. 1840 aged 25 yrs. Claim #10693: $44.00.

Andrews, Ambrose — Res.: Lenox. Major in the 74th Regt. First town clerk in 1810; Joined Sullivan F. & A. M. Lodge in 1804.

Annis, Truman — Res.: Nelson. 129th Regt.; Claim #5858: $40.00. Lived in Fond du Lac, WI.

Armour, Preston — Res.: Smithfield. b. 1794 - d. 1879.

Auchenpaauch, Rudolphus — Res.: Sullivan. Claim #6505: $41.50.

Averhill, Henry K.	Res: Morrisville. Pension Certificate No. 13, $8.00 per mo. 1883.
Avery, Clark	Res.: Fenner; d. 13 July 1859 aged 67 yrs.; buried in Perryville. Claim # 10701: $38.50.
Avery, Shuman	d. 7 October 1860 aged 64 yrs., bur. in Merrilsville.
Ayers, Joseph	Res.: Cazenovia. Lt in 129th Regt. On jury in Nelson 1829. d. 15 Dec. 1830, age 40 yrs.
Ayres, Perley	Res: Eaton. 65th Regt. Had a woolen mill.
Babcock, John	Res.: Hamilton. Pvt. in the Artillery.
Babcock, Oliver	Res.: Brookfield. Vet. 143rd Regt. Claim #7631: $20.00.
Babcock, Phineas	Res: Brookfield (Bridgewater, Chenango Co ?). d. 12 April 1857 age 79 yrs.
Bacon, Levi, Jr.	Res.: DeRuyter Claim #10710: $58.00 & #5960: $58.00. Buried New Woodstock; b. 1894, d. 1861.
Bacon, Levi, Sr.	Res: Hamilton; Claim #1568: $39.00.
Bacon, Philemon	Res.: Hamilton. Sgt. in 143rd Regt.; d. 1864 age 81 yrs. Claim #2084: $70.00 [He applied for pension but it was denied as he was enlisted under the name "Lemon" when his real name was Philemon. His pension application is long and unusually interesting. Ed.]
Bailey, Lewis	Served in a corps of Riflemen. Claim #3482: $73.00; moved to Monroe, MI.
Ballou, Arnold	Res.: Fenner. Commissioned Officer. Buried in a private

Ballou - continued	cemetery on his farm on the east side of road a short distance north of Fenner Four Corners; b. 1772 - d. 1833. [This cemetery had been all but destroyed by animals pastured therein when last seen by the editor in 1959.]
Barber, Elihu	Res.: Eaton. Veteran of the 56th Regt.; Constable in 1809.
Barber, Ezekiel	Res: Stockbridge; d. 25 Dec. 1868 aged 75 yrs.; buried on East Hill; Claim #2542. $28.00. Res. in Cazenovia.
Barber, John	Settled in Fenner in 1799; had the 1st potashery in the town; d. 30 Nov. 1869 aged 95 yrs.; bur. at Fenner Corners. Claim # 2407, $46.00.
Barker, Dr. Daniel	Res.: Madison; joined Medical Soc. in 1820; Claim # 15582 - $55.00 & #12132 - $58.00. Moved to Macomb., St. Lawrence Co. NY. Res. at time of 2nd claim given as Rossie, St. Lawrence Co.
Barker, Rutherford	Quartermaster 3rd Artillery. Lived in Madison, d. 30 Nov. 1838, aged 80 yrs.
Barker, Silas	Res. given only as Madison Co.; Claim #5971: $58.00.
Barnard, Horace	[Son of?] David; b. at Quality Hill; lived at Canastota in 1835.
Barnes, Leverett	Res.: Bridgeport; Lt. in Beecher's Co. at Sacketts Harbor; moved to IL.
Barrett, William P.	Res.: Peterboro; d. 1868 aged 73 yrs.; Served while living in CT.
Bartholomay, Andrew	Fifer in Beecher's Co. at Sacketts Harbor.

Batcheller, Nathaniel	Res.: Lincoln.
Bates, Obediah	Res.: Lincoln; Pvt. in Beecher's Co. at Sackett's Harbor.
Beach, Backus	Res.: Eaton; b. 1782, d. 1864.
Beckwith, Daniel	Res.: Morrisville; d. 23 Aug 1816 age 33 yrs.
Beckwith, James	Res.: Cazenovia. Claim #1399: $47.00. Pensioned at $8.00 per month in 1883.
Beckwith, Roswell	b. 1761 d. 1836. Commissioned officer in the 129th Regt.; also served in the Revolution; Pensioned in 1832. War of 1812 Claim #1402: $47.00.
Bedford, Stephen	Res.: Clockville. Moved to northern New York.
Beebe, Elihu	Lt. in the 65th Regt.
Beebe, James	Res.: Sullivan; d. 27 Feb 1865 age 77 yrs.; 74th Regt. Claim #8170: $63.00.
Beebe, John	Res.: Lenox; Served in the 3rd Artillery.
Beebe, Silas, Jr.	Res.: Hamilton; Adj. to Maj. Gen. Claim #268: $24.50. Moved to Newport, Herkimer Co. NY.
Beebe, William	Res.: Sullivan; served in the 74th Regt.
Beecher, Alfred	Drummer in Beecher's Co. at Sacketts Harbor.
Beecher, Daniel	Res.: Lenox.
Beecher, David	Res.: Sullivan; Cornet in the Artillery.
Beecher, James	Son [of] Walter lived in Lenox; d. in U. S. service in War of
Beecher, James-cont'd	1812. Estate settled in 1822.

Beecher, Sylvester	1771-1849; res.: Lincoln. Bur. at Canastota; raised a company and served as a Capt. at Sacketts' Harbor.
Beecher, William H.	Res.: Sullivan. Sgt. in Beecher's Co. at Sackett's Harbor. Claim #W297: $41.50. [Moved to] Howard, NY or Orwell, NY?].
Bellinger, Simon	Res: Sullivan; Pvt. in Beecher's Co. at Sacketts Harbor.
Benedict, Nathan	Claim #2802: $38.00. Res. is given as Georgetown, Madison Co.; d. 14 Oct. 1866
Benedict, Samuel	Res.: Cazenovia. Claim #6590: $58.00 & #393; $65.00.
Benjamin, Elias	Capt., pensioned in 1823 at $72.00 per year, for service in War of 1812; Served in the 16th NY Militia; lived in DeRuyter; d. 26 Nov. 1866.
Benjamin, John	Res.: Lenox; Claim # 6590: $58.00.
Bennett, David	Served in a battalion of Riflemen; Claim #7769: $58.50. Removed to Cairo, Greene Co., NY.
Benson, Harry	Res: Cazenovia (Sullivan), Madison Co.; Claim #4375; $50.00.
Bentley, William, Jr.	Res.: Cazenovia; Ensign in the 129th Regt.; Claim #1441 by widow living in Erie Co., PA. $55.00.
Berry, Daniel	Res.: Lenox in 1837; Pvt. in Beecher's Co. at Sacketts Harbor.
Berry, Ephriam	Res.: Brookfield; 143rd Regt.
Berthrong, James	8th Co. ?
Bicknell, Bennett	Res.: Morrisville; 1781-1841.

Bierge (Burge), Chancellor	Res.: Randallsville. Pensioned in 1883 at $8.00 per mo.; Claim #10659: $58.00
Biggs, Benjamin	Pvt. in 74th Regt.
Biggs, William	Pvt. in 74th Regt.
Blair, Alvin A.	Res.: Nelson. Cl. #10872: $20.00. 1796-1883, bur. in Cazenovia.
Blair, Enoch	Res.: Nelson. 1771 -1834.
Blair, Jeremiah	Res.: Nelson. Claim #4924: $46.00. 1795 -1878.
Blakeslee, Asa	Res.: Perryville; d. 8 March 1860 age 77 yrs.
Blakeslee, David	Res.: Morrisville [town of Eaton?]. Claim #853: $72.00. d. Mar. 1868 age 76 yrs.
Blanchard, Walter	Res.: Hamilton. Claim #1519: $39.00. d. 13 Feb. 1879 age 84 yrs., bur. in Poolville.
Blanding Ebenezer	Lt. in 65th Regt.
Bond, Elijah	b. 1769, settled in Hamilton 1797; d. 20 October 1844, bur. in N.W. (New Woodstock?). Claim #5962: $25.00.
Bond, Marble	Claim #1565: $39.00. d. 1 September 1864 age 72 yrs; bur. at Madison Lake.
Bonney, Barnabus	Served in the 65th Regt.
Bonney, Benjamin	Res: Hamilton; Ensign in the 65th Regt.; Claim #1875: $65.00. d. 1868 age 86 yrs., bur. in Georgetown.
Bonney, Heman	?
Bonney, Thomas	Res: Hamilton; Ensign in the 65th Regt.

Bort, Henry	Res.: Clockville. Sgt. in Beecher's Co. at Sacketts Harbor. b. 1783.
Bort, Nicholas N.	Res: Clockville; served in the 74th Regt. b. 1788, d. 1868; bur. Hastings, NY.
Boyer, Adam	Res.: Clockville; Pvt. in Beecher's Co. at Sacketts Harbor.
Bridge, William	Lived in Stockbridge; served in 3rd Artillery; d. 27 Jan. 1877 age 82 yrs.
Briggs, Hugh	Res.: Sullivan. 74th Regt.
Briggs, Phineas	Res.: Fenner; Commissioned Officer in the 129th Regt.; Claim #7056: $55.00. Moved to Ridgeway, NY.
Briggs, Thomas	Claim #2313: $55.00. Shoemaker; b. 1791 - d.1881; buried in Clockville.
Bronson, Rueben	Served in the 74th Regt.
Bronson, Westel	Res: Hamilton; Claim #1457: $41.00.
Brown, Daniel F.	Res: Sullivan; Claim #90; $14.00; pensioned at $8.00 per month in 1883. Lived at Bridgeport.
Brown, Francis	Served in a Batt. of Riflemen; Claim #15818: $63.00; moved to Niagara Co., NY.
Brown, John	Res.: Sullivan; served in 74th Regt.; Claim #7691: $58.00; Moved to Winnibago Co., WI.
Brown, John	Res: Hamilton; Cornet in the Artillery; Claim #15356: $55.00. Lived Rockton, IL.
Brown, Lorey	Res: Smithfield; Claim #13792: $55.00.

Brown, Minor	Capt. 8th Cavalry; Lot 31, Lincoln 1820.
Brown, Simeon	Res: Brookfield; Chaplain of the 143rd Regt.; d. 1826.
Brown, Solomon	Res.: Sullivan; Pvt. 3rd Art. Claim #16459: $55.00; Wife, Elizabeth d. 25 Mar. 1854 age 54 yrs; bur. at Chittenango.
Brown, William	Lt. in 8th Cavalry; Claim #9624: $50.00; res.: Genesee Co., MI.
Brown, William	129th Regt. War Claim #7082: $20.00; moved to Manlius.
Bruce, Joseph	Res.: Lenox; Lt. in Light Artillery; 1789-1872; buried at Quality Hill, [Town of Lincoln].
Bull, Luman	Res.: Lincoln; 74th Regt.; 1786-1858; bur. at Quality Hill, [town of Lincoln].
Bumpus, Benjamin	Res.: Nelson. Lt. in the 129th Regt.
Burch, Nathan	143rd Regt.; Res.: Brookfield.
Burdick, Benjamin	143rd Regt.; d. 26 July 1876 age 80 yrs.; bur. at W. Edmeston.
Burgess, Levi	Res.: Cazenovia; Claim #5955: $28.95. 1773-1862.
Burr, William G.	Res : Cazenovia; Claim #1405: $75.00; d. 5 Aug. 1860, age 69; bur. Cazenovia.
Burton, Charles	Res.: Cazenovia; d. 11 Mar 1842, age 66 yrs.; bur. Hardscrabble Cem.; had son, Joseph.
Burton, John E.	Res.: Madison Co. Claim #5952: $58.00.
Burton, Rodney (Robert)	Res.: Cazenovia. Claim #15295: $53.00. [n.b.: A Robert Burton is listed in the official record but his residence is given as Sullivan Co. NY]

Butler, Daniel	Res: Stockbridge; Claim #855: $80.00.
Button, George W.	Res: Brookfield; Claim #1503: $58.00.
Button, Joseph C.	
Byer, Nicholas	Res.: Hamilton; Claim #2095: $60.00 and # 2096: $30.00
Cady, Angelus	Res.: Sullivan; Lt. Artillery
Cady, Asa W.	Res.: Lenox; Capt. and Chief of Staff of Engineers. 1779-1854, bur. in Chittenango.
Cadwell, Ebenezer G.	(Caldwell?) Res: Lenox and Sullivan; moved to Crystal Lake, IA; 1787-1879.
Camp, Abner, Jr.	Res.: Eaton; served in corps of Riflemen.
Campbell, Adam	Res.: Eaton; Claim #5953: $74.00; Wife, Anna lived in Eaton.
Campbell, James	Pensioned 16 Apr. 1816 at $48.00 p.a.; d. 7 Sept 1827; Served in Col. Topham's Regt.; transferred from VT 4 Sept 1824.
Campbell, Moses	Served in 56th Regt.; wife d. 21 Mar 1819 age 36 yrs., bur. at Poolville.
Campbell, Nicholas	Pvt. in Beechers Co.; Claim #8932: $70.00 by Admns.
Campbell, Richard	Res.: Sullivan in 1820, Smithfield in 1821; Pvt. in Beechers Co.; blacksmith.
Carhart, Tristan	Settled in Canastota in 1805; Ensign in the 74th Regt.
Carpenter, Elijah	Res.: Erieville; shoemaker; 1775-1843.
Carscadden, John	Res.: Stockbridge; #19636;

Carscadden - cont'd	$8.00 per month; d. 23 July 1881 age 90 yrs.
Carter, John	Res.: Sullivan; Claim #15571: $60.00
Cary, Thomas	Served in 3rd Artillery.
Case, Grandly	Res: Nelson; Claim #873: $41.00 & #10695: $47.00.
Case, Jeremiah	Son of George...
Case, Ozias	Res.: Lenox; Fifer in Beechers Co. at Sacketts Harbor.
Cazier, John Le Conte	Physician in Lebanon; 1790-1863; buried near Lebanon Reservoir.
Chadwick, Isaac	Sgt. 129th Regt.; 1788-1868; buried near Madison Lake.
Chandler, Orin	Res.: Cazenovia; served in 129th Regt.
Champlin, Edward	Res: Brookfield; d. 17 Sept. 1865 age 75 yrs.
Chapin, Ezra	Served in 65th Regt., Claim #14133: $55.00 by admns.; d. Prattsburg, NY.
Chapin, Roswell	Served in 143rd Regt.; d. 6 Dec 1830; wife, Delight was bur. in Brookfield.
Chapman, John	Lived in Sullivan on New Boston St.; served in the 129th Regt.; d. 27 June 1831.
Chapman, Nathan	b. in CT 1786; served at Stonington, CT; settled south of Clockville on the Mt. Pleasant farm in 1815; died at Auburn, NY 27 June 1871.
Chapman, Stephen	Res: Clockville; Ensign in the 74th Regt.; Claim #2314 (no amount given); 1785-1862.
Chappell. Peter	Served with the 65th Regt; d.

Chappell - cont'd.	7 April 1813?, age 33; buried at Poolville.
Cheesebro, Christopher	Res.: Brookfield or Columbus, NY ?; d. 18 Sept 1876 age 84 yrs.
Cheesbro, James	Res.: Brookfield; served with 143rd Regt.
Childs, Perry G.	Res.: Cazenovia; served on staff of Gen. Hurd; d. 27 Mar 1835 age 56 yrs.; bur. Fenner St., Cazenovia.
Clark, Benjamin	[Tarbox?] Res: Cazenovia; Claim #1392: $47.00; 1797-1875.
Clark, David	Res.: Brookfield; Cornet; d. 24 Feb. 1863 age 77 yrs.
Clark, Eliakim	Res. DeRuyter; Claim #1393: $47.50 & #10709: $41.50; helped build the New Woodstock Church in 1815.
Clark, Ethan	Res: Brookfield; Adjutant; d. 18 June 1869 age 86 yrs.; wife, Polly.
Clark, Henry	Res.: Brookfield; Chaplain, 143rd Regt; d. 1831 age 74 yrs.
Clark, James B.	Res.: Brookfield; Ensign in the 143rd Regt.
Clark, Jasper	Res: Hamilton; Capt. in the 65th Regt.
Clark, Norman	Res.: Lenox; Capt. in the 74th Regt.; d. 25 May 1859; bur. at Quality Hill
Clark, Samuel B.	Res.: Brookfield. Cornet.
Clark, Thomas	Res: Sullivan; Capt. in the 74th Regt.; Claim #16310: $50.00 by widow; d. 14 March 1844 age 64 yrs.
Claus, Jasper	Commissioned officer on staff of the 35th Brigade.

Cleveland, Erasmus	Res.: Madison; Col. in the 65th Regt; 1771-1844.
Cleveland, Ephriam	Served in 129th Regt.; lived in Sullivan and DeRuyter; d. 1814; Claim #16510: $65.00; Naples, NY.
Cleveland, John	Res.: Stockbridge; 129th Regt.; Claim #1354: $59.00. Res: Clymer, NY.
Cleveland, William P.	Res.: Madison; Surg. 56th Regt; 1779-1858; Res.: Madison
Clock. John, Jr.	Res.: Clockville; 74th Regt.; d. 12 March 1835; buried in Central Square, NY.
Clock, Joseph, 2nd	Claim #663: $48.50; b. 1785; d. between 1870-1874; moved to Hastings, Oswego Co., NY.
Clock, Peter	Res.: Clockville; Claim #3311: $55.00; 1795-1862; Lived in Oneida Co. in 1835.
Coats, Billings	Res.: Brookfield; 1st term [of service?] Claim #2741: $108.00; 2 term, #2741, $58.00.
Coats (Cotes), Ebenezer	Ensign in the 129th Regt.; [b.] 1773 - d. 5 Mar. 1862; bur. New Woodstock.
Cobb, Henry	Res.: Madison Co.; also postmaster at Chittenango; Claim #2148: $75.00.
Cobb, Daniel	Capt. in the 129th Regt.
Coburn, Stephen	Res.: Cazenovia; Served in 129th Regt.; d. 13 March 1829; wife, Polly, son, ·Loren.
Coe, Isaac	Res: Madison; 1772 - 1841.
Coe, Jabez	Res: Stockbridge; served while living in Oneida Co. NY
Coe, John	Res.: Stockbridge.

Coleman, Stephen	Res.: Cazenovia; Capt. in the 129th Regt.; d. 1870.
Collins, Nathaniel	Res.: Hamilton; Brig. Gen., 35th Brigade; d. 22 July 1824, age 50 yrs.; bur. at Earlville.
Collister, Marsena	Claim #861: $40.00; 1st white child b. in the town of Madison.
Collister, Samuel	Ensign in the 65th Regt.; wife, Betsey d. 30 July 1832, age 67 yrs.; she was buried at Madison Lake.
Colton, Warren	Res.: Canastota; served in the 3rd Artillery.
Coman, Winsor	Res.: Town of Eaton. 1776-1861. Bur. at Morrisville.
Conger, Parley	Res.: Lenox; Claim #16686: $65.00; d. 6 May 1865 age 77 yrs.; bur. at Whitelaw.
Cook, Moses	Adj. 74th Regt. d. 1825, bur. Quality Hill. (town of Lenox), no g.s. Had son, Chauncey.
Cool, Daniel	Res: Sullivan. War Claim: #5414: $20.00.
Cooley, George	129th Regt.
Coonrad, Adam.	Res.: Sullivan. Claim # 16460 by his widow, $55.00.
Covenhoven, John A.	Res.: Georgetown. Claim #2801: $53.00.
Covill, Asa	Res.: Cazenovia. Served in 8th Cavalry.
Cowan, William	Claim # 1526: $65.00. Res. given as Madison Co.
Crandall, Sanders	Res.: Brookfield. 143rd Regt.
Cranson, Cabel	Res.: Lincoln. Ensign in 74th Regt.

Cranson, Elisha	Res.: Lincoln. Ensign in 74th Regt.; moved to Michigan.
Cranson, Martin	Res.: Clockville, 1788-1843.
Crary, Gideon K.	Res.: Lincoln; b. 1793 in CT; owned the Chaffee farm in town of Lincoln; Claim #6593: $50.00.
Crocker, Oliver	Res.: Cazenovia. Lt. in 129th Regt.
Crocker, Wilbur	(Webber?) Res.: Cazenovia. Lt. in 129th Regt.
Cross, Calvin	Res.: Eaton; b. 1781 - d. 23 Feb. 1868; bur. in Georgetown; Claim #5967: $41.50.
Crouse, George	Res.: Canastota; Claim #12295: $31.50.
Culver, Richard	Res: Cazenovia; 129th Regt.; Claim #2171: $100.00.
Culver, Submit	Res.: Chittenango Falls; Pensioned at $8.00 per month in 1883.
Cunningham, James J.	d. 17 Dec. 1813 ae 39 yrs.; bur. at Earlville.
Curtis, Japhlet	Pvt. in the 5th U. S. Infantry. Pensioned $48.00 p.a. for service in the War of 1812 on Aug. 6, 1834.
Curtis, William J.	Capt. in the 65th Regt.; Tavern Keeper at Madison.
Cypher, Andrew	Res.: Lincoln. 1779-1831; bur. in the old Buyea Cem. Claim #2318: $58.00.
Dalrymph, John	Res.: Brookfield; Lt. in 143rd Regt.
Danby, Lewis H.	74th Regt.; Agent for the Lenox Iron Co.
Daniels, Erasmus	Served with 65th Regt.; d. 1819 age 41 yrs.; bur. at Earlville.

Darling, Alpheus	65th Regt.; d. 8 Dec. 1838 ae 65 yrs; bur. at Madison.
Davis, Isaac	Res.: Fenner; 1764-1824; bur. west of Codys Corner; also a veteran of the Rev. War.
Davis, Nathaniel	Res: Erieville; d. 8 Sept. 1846 ae 58 yrs.
Davison, John	Capt. in 129th Regt.; res: Cazenovia; d. 1815; wife, Polly.
Day, Charles	Res: Brookfield; Ensign in the 143rd Regt.
Dean, Anson	Res: Cazenovia; settled in 1793; 129th Regt.
Dean, John	Res: Eaton; 1786-1847; Claim # 5329: $58.00 by Admns.
Decker, Michael P.	Served with Beecher's Co. at Sacketts Harbor.
Denna, Andrew	Res.: Hamilton; Claim #8820: $95.00.
Denner, Jesse	Res: Sullivan; Pvt. in Beecher's Co. at Sacketts Harbor.
Dennison, Asa	Res. Brookfield; 143rd Regt.
Denton, Abner	Res: Hamilton; Claim #8821: $52.00 by Admns.
Dewey, Noah	Res.: Oneida; Claim #5370: $55.00 by widow.
Dexter, Smith	Served in the 129th Regt; moved to Independence, Cattaraugus Co., NY; Claim #7840: $44.00.
Dick, Levi	Res.: Madison; 65th Regt. 1785-1870.
Dinehart, Jeremiah	Res.: Sullivan; Claim #16877: $55.00 by his widow.
Dodge, Isaac	Res.: Cazenovia; Claim #1396: $70.00.

Dodge, Stephen	Res.: Cazenovia; Capt. in the 129th Regt; d. 20 Feb. 1848 ae 83 yrs.
Dorn, John I.	Res: Smithfield; d. 18 June 1869 ae 74 yrs; Claim #5951: $11.50.
Douglass, Zebulon	Res.: Sullivan; d. 12 July 1849 ae 80 yrs., bur. Quality Hill; Col. in the 74th Regt.
Dryer, Wheeler	Res.: Georgetown; owned a sawmill ; Claim #1876 - $65.00.
Duncan, Seth	Res.: Brookfield; served with the 143rd Regt.
Dunham, Isaac	65th Regt.; Claim # 1752: $14.00; Lived at Stephentown [Rensselaer Co.], NY.
Duncan, Jonas	Res.: Madison; Claim #2657: $26.00.
Dwight, J. H.	Res.: Brookfield; Commissioned in U.S. Army during War of 1812.
Dye, William	Res: Brookfield; Cornet in 143rd Regt.
Dygert, Henry	One of earliest settlers at Oneida; Res: Lenox; Claim #15675 - $55.00 by exec.
Dykeman, Czar	Res.: Fenner; d. 4 Feb. 1841 age 54 yrs.; bur. Perryville.
Eaton, DeStang	Cornet in 143rd Regt.
Eddy, William	Res: Lenox. (Chittenango?); Claim #-238: $58.00 by admns; d. 22 Apr. 1854 ae 75 yrs. bur. Merrillsville.
Eggleson, Asa	Served with the 129th Regt.
Ehle, Henry	Res.: Chittenango; Claim #16027: $58.00.
Eldridge, James B.	Served with 3rd Artillery; d. 15 Sept. 1864 age 79 yrs.; bur. Earlville.

Elliott, Smith	129th Regt.; Claim #7263: $39.50; Res.: Lenawee Co., MI.
Ellis, David	Pvt. in Beecher's Co. at Sacketts Harbor; Claim #4253: $54.00 by admns.; Moved to Westmoreland, Oneida Co.
Emerson, Ephriam P.	Res.: Lebanon; Claim #14845: $13.00.
Enos, David C.	Res: Eaton; d. 28 Oct 1877 age 86 yrs.
Enos, John	Lt. in the 65th Regt.
Ensley, William	Res.: Hamilton; Claim #1383: $60.00.
Farnham, Elisha	Res.: Cazenovia; Col. in the 129th Regt. at Sacketts Harbor; 1768-1848; bur. at Cazenovia.
Farrington, Charles	Res.: Sullivan; Claim #15570: $55.00.
Fetterly, John A.	Res.: Stockbridge; Claim #5242 by Admns., $38.50.
Fink, John J.	Res.: Chittenango; served with the 74th Regt.
Fiske, Silas	Res. Sullivan; Claim #88: $28.00.
Fiske, William E.	Res. Canastota; served in MA; came to Madison Co. in 1822; b. 1796 - d. 25 Nov. 1873.
Fitch, Derick H.	Res.: Peterboro; Capt.; Claim #1406: $52.00; b. 1798; d. 14 Sept 1879; bur. in Cazenovia.
Fletcher, Stillman	Res.: Eaton; Claim #6968: $58.00.
Forbes, Bartholomay	Claim #6177: $43.00; 1792 - 1879; d. Conneaut, PA.
Forbes, Bartholomay	Res.: Clockville; 1784-1860.

Forbes, John	Res.: Clockville; 74th Regt.; Claim #16170 by widow; $65.00.
Forbes, John (Scotch)	Res.: Lenox. Claim #2316; $38.50; 1783 - 1860.
Forbes, Nicholas J.	Pvt. in Beecher's Co; moved to MI.
Forbes, Nicholas I.	Pvt. in Beecher's Co. [at Sacketts Harbor]; Claim #13518: $55.00; d. Warren Co., PA in 1844.
French, Samuel	Res.: Chittenango; served at Ft. Erie.
Frink, Enoch	Res.: Eaton. Claim #13791: $38.00; 1783-1872
Foster, Thomas	Res.: Brookfield; d. 14 May 1844 age 74 yrs.
Fox, Dennison	Served in 8th Cavalry.
Fuller, Joseph	Res. Hamilton. Claim #1523: $22.00; d. 1 June 1856 age 79 years; bur. Hubbardsville.
Gage, Samuel	Res.: Eaton; Claim #867: $15.00; Died in DeRuyter 19 Feb 1868 age 78 yrs.
Gale, John	Res.: Oneida; father of W. Hector Gale, Oneida publisher.
Gaston, Chauncy	Res.: Eaton; later lived in Whitelaw in town of Lenox; served in 65th Regt.
Gaylord, Edward L.	Son-in-law of Gen. Cleveland.
Gear, Nathan	d. 24 May 1849 age 84 yrs., bur. at Earlville; also served in the Revolutionary War in the 3rd. Regt. Militia at Preston, CT.
Gibbs, John	Res.: Madison; Claim #5373; $55.00.
Gilbert, William	Res. Brookfield; Claim #4223; $76.50.

Gilmore, Arunda (Arunah?) Sr.	[served or Sgt.?] in Bicknell's Batt. of Riflemen; d. 30 Aug 1855 age 62 yrs.; bur. at Madison.
Goodell, Calvin	Res.: Sullivan; served in the 74th Regt.
Goodell, John, Jr.	Lt. in 65th Regt. Claim #9448; $30.00; juryman in Cazenovia in 1813; Moved to Decatur, NY.
Goodwin, Samuel N.	Res.: Lincoln; Claim #14018: $67.00; moved to Dodge Co., WI.
Gorton, Samuel	Res. Brookfield; Claim #8590: $30.00;
Gorton, Wanton	Res: Brookfield. Claim #13052: $30.00; 28 Feb. 1860 age 63 yrs.
Gray, Collister	Lived near Hamilton; served with the 65th Regt.
Gray, Ephriam	Served with the 65 Regt.; d. 21 Feb 1851 age 71 yrs.; bur in Lebanon.
Gray, John	Res: Sullivan; Claim #9159: $20.00.
Green, Aaron	Res: Brookfield; 43rd Regt (143rd?).
Green, Peter	Res: Nelson; Claim #871: $60.00.
Greenly, Thomas H.	Res. ; Hamilton; Commissioned officer in the 65th Regt.; Claim #1382: $39.00; d. 1 Aug 1832; wife, Mary.
Gregg, William T.	Res.: Stockbridge; Claim #862: $42.00.
Gridley, Timothy	Res: Cazenovia; Col. in the Militia.
Griffin, Robert	Res.: Eaton; Claim #5957: $41.50; d. 12 Aug. 1872, age 88 yrs.; bur. Pine Woods.

Griggs, Bradford	Res: Eaton; Claim #372: $15.00; lived in Lenox in 1835.
Gumall, Bradford	Pvt. in Beecher's Co. at Sacketts Harbor.
Guston, Jabez	Res. Hamilton; Claim #1525: $57.00.
Haight, Isaac	Served in 65th Regt.
Hall, Nathaniel	Served as a sgt. in 74th Regt.; 1781-1870; bur. at Quality Hill.
Hall, Solomon	d. Rochester, NY 31 March 1860 age 60 yrs.; bur. Quality Hill. Claim #4240; $54.25.
Hall, Stephen R.	Served as an Ensign.
Hall, Timothy	Served in the 8th Cavalry.
Hamilton, John	Res.: Nelson; Claim #876: $47.00 & #10694: $47.00.
Hardendorf, John	Pvt. in Beecher's Co. at Sacketts Harbor.
Harding, Horace	Drummer in Beecher's Co. at Sacketts Harbor.
Harrington, Stephen	Res.: Wampsville; Pvt. in Beecher's Co. at Sacketts Harbor.
Harrison, Benjamin	Res.: Sullivan; Commissioned officer.
Hartshorn, Jacob	Capt. in 65th Regt.; d. 1850 age 72 yrs. Res: Lebanon.
Hartshorn, John	Res.: Lebanon; Claim #6504: $41.00; moved to Syracuse, NY.
Harp. George, Jr.	Res.: Clockville; Claim #8071; $58.50. Pvt. in Beecher's Co. at Sacketts Harbor; b. 1798; also lived at Verona, NY.
Hatch, John	Served in 65th Regt.; Claim #14992: $55.00; moved to Brookhaven, NY.

Hatch, Zena	Res.: Madison; Lt.; wife, Sally d. 12 June 1864 age 74 yrs.
Hathway, Luther	Res.: Stockbridge; later moved to Augusta (Oneida Co); served at Sacketts Harbor; b. 21 Oct 1793, d. 16 Dec 1882.
Havens Nathaniel	Res.: DeRuyter; Capt. in 65th Regt.; Claim #2546: $75.00; moved to Big Flats, NY (Chemung Co.).
Hays, John	Res.: Sullivan; Claim #89: $55.00.
Hayword, Ransom	Res.: Hamilton and Lebanon; Claim #1380: $39.00.
Hazzard, Paul	Res.: Madison, Lot #55; Inspector of beef and Pork for the army.
Hearsay, John	Res.: Cazenovia; served with the 129th Regt.; distiller; d. 1871.
Heffron, Aabner	Served in a corps of Rifleman.
Heffron, John	Res.: Nelson; Sgt. Beeknells (Bucknell's) Corps; Claim #5960: $41.50; d. 20 May 1861 age 73 yrs, bur. at Erieville.
Hemstraight, Richard	Pvt. in Beechers Co, at Sacketts Harbor.
Henry, Robert	Served with the 65th Regt; Eaton merchant.
Herrick, Smith	Res.- Lenox - later moved to Onondaga Co.; 3rd Artillery; Claim #13821: $55.00
Hicks, John F.	Supervisor of the town of Brookfield 1837.
Hill, Eli F.	Res: Cazenovia; Lt. in 3th Cavalry.
Hills, Silah	Res.: Lenox.

Holmes, Benjamin	Res: Cazenovia; Claim #1126: $100.00.
Holmes, Israel	Claim #2098: $45.00; b. 1781 - d. at Hamilton 1865; bur. at Hubbardsville.
Holmes, Jabez	Res.: Hamilton. Claim #2098: $45.00
Holmes, Samuel	Res: Cazenovia; 129th Regt.; Claim #13253: $73.00; moved to Brocton, Chautauqua Co., NY.
Hoppin (Hopkin?)	Res.: Lebanon; 1785-1868.
Holton, Rufus	Res.: Brookfield; Sgt. in 143rd Regt.
House, James	Res: Madison; Capt. in U. S. Regt; d. 1834.
Howard, Albert	d. 28 July 1864 age 76 yrs.; bur. at Pine Woods.
Howard, John	Res.: Eaton. Claim #5954: $41.50
Howes, Herman	Res.: Madison Co.; Claim #1385: $39.00
Hubbard, Samuel	Served in 129th Regt.
Huntley, James	Res. Oneida Valley; pensioned at $8.00 per month in 1883; 1795-1885.
Hurd, Ezra	Res.: Georgetown; Capt. in 129th Regt.
Hurd, Asa	Claim #887: $60.00; d. at Greece, Monroe Co., bur. Perryville - no dates on stone.
Hurd, Jabez	Res.: Cazenovia; Brig. Gen.; d. at Albany.
Hutchinson, John	Res.: Fenner; Lt. in the 129th Regt.
Hutchinson, Loring	d. 26 Aug 1860 age 72 yrs; bur. Mutton Hill [Muttonville, Ont.

Loring – cont'd	Co.?]; Col.in the Militia; Claim #10713: $47.00 & #2138: $8.00 by admns.
Hyde, Daniel	Res.: Brookfield; 143rd Regt.; Claim #1504: $55.00.
Hynds, Christopher	Res.: Sullivan; Claim #87: $61.00.
Ingraham, Abel	Res.: Stockbridge; Claim #874: $51.00; d. 26 May 1860 age 70 yrs.
Jackson, Elijah	Claim #14864: $21.00; d. 15 June 1854; bur. at Sheds; no age on stone.
Jackson, John	65th Regt.; Claim #14047: $55.00; moved to Stueben Co., IN.
Jackson, Seliathiel	Major in the 129th Regt.
Jacques, Samuel	Res.: Hamilton. Claim #1502 $63.00
James, Almeron	Pvt. in 13th Regt. U.S Regular [Army]; d. 27 April 1813; heirs: Alphilede, Mary, Emeline, Louisa, Diantha, & James allowed $48.00 per year for 5 yrs. service from 20 May 1820-18 March 1825.
Jencks, Elmore	Res.: DeRuyter; rose to be a Col. in a Regt. of Militia.; b. 1791.
Jennings, Uriah	Corp. in CT Militia in 1814; d. 10 January, 1832, age 70 yrs.; bur. at Whitelaw; wife, Ruth.
Keeler, Lewis	Res.: Smithfield and Fenner; d. 4 Nov. 1846 age 58 yrs.; bur. Cazenovia; Claim #4310: $46.50.
Kern, George	Res.: Lincoln; 74th Regt.; rose to Capt.
Kern, Jacob	Res.: Lenox; Pvt. in Beecher's

Kern – cont'd	Co. at Sacketts Harbor; Claim #15524: $55.00. b. 1878; moved to Ashippen, Dodge Co., WI.
Kern, John M.	Res.: Clockville; Pvt. with Beecher's Co. at Sacketts Harbor.
Keys, Shubal	Res.: Stockbridge.
Kill[t?], George	Res.: Lenox; Pvt. in Beecher's Co. at Sacketts Harbor; Claim #5182: $33.50; moved to Lysander, Onondaga Co, NY.
Kilts, Conrad, Jr.	b. 1789; Res.: Clockville; Pvt. in Beechers Co. at Sacketts Harbor.
Kilts, Nicholas	1792-1864; Res. Clockville; Pvt in Beecher's Co. at Sacketts Harbor; Claim #3312: $70.00.
Kitts, Christian	(Kilts?) 1791-1867; Res.: Clockville; Claim #6591: $75.00.
Kimball, John	Pvt. in Beecher's Co. at Sacketts Harbor; Claim #2282: $46.00; moved to Milford, NY.
King, Nathaniel	1767-1848; Res. Hamilton; Maj. General of the 6th Div.
Knapp, Aaron	Res.: Eaton. Claim #5241: $38.50.
Kneiss, Thomas Y.	1778-1854; bur. Quality Hill. 74th Regt.
Knight, Henry	1797-1865; bur. Morrisville.
Lamb, Amos	Res.: Brookfield; 143 Regt.
Lamb, Martin	1781 - 1846; Res.: Lincoln; bur. Perryville.
Lamb, Seth	Pvt. in Bicknell's Corps of Riflemen.
Ladeu, Ezekiel	Res.: Eaton; Claim #223: $54.00.

La Munion, David	Res.: Stockbridge.
Lathrop, John	Served in 129th Regt.; became a lawyer in Peterboro.
Leach, Backus	Res.: Eaton; d. 1864 age 82 yrs.
Ledyard, Jonathan	Res.: Cazenovia; served in 129th Regt.; 1793-1874.
Lee, John	Res: Sullivan; 74th Regt.; Claim #14041: $58.00 by Admns, Luzerne Co., PA.
Lee Joseph	Lt. in 74th Regt.; d. 18 Nov 1847 age 63 yrs.; bur. New Boston St., [town of] Lenox.
Lee, Stephen	1780-1842; Bur. N. Boston St.; Capt. in 74th Regt.
Leland, Uriah	Res.: Eaton; settled in 1794; d. prior to 1850; served in 3rd Art.; Claim #5240: $58.00 by admns.
Leonard, Rev. Lewis	Res: Cazenovia; d. 1 Nov 1856 age 71 yrs; Chaplain of the 129th regt.
Leonard, Rueben	Res.: Brookfield; Col. in 43rd Regt.
Lester, Henry R.	8th Cavalry.
Lewis, Isaac	1782-1879; res.: Eaton; 1st Lt. Horse Artillery.
Lewis, Jeremiah	143rd Regt. Claim #6759: $14.00; moved to Ellisburg, NY.
Lickley, Oliver	Ensign in 65th Regt.
Lincklaen, John	1777-1847; res.: Cazenovia.
Littlefield, Elijah	Res.: Cazenovia; Maj. in 8th Cavalry.
Livermore, Sameul	Served in the 143rd Regt.
Loomis, Calvin	Res.: Hubbardsville; d. 1 June 1859 age 66 yrs.

Loomis, George	Res.: Eaton; Claim #14543: $55.00 and 7539: 60.50. Claim gives res. as Lebanon.
Loomis, Isaac	Res.: Brookfield. Lt. in 143rd Regt.
Loomis, Lyman	Res: Eaton. Claim #6668: $50.00 and #6672: $50.00
Lord, William	Res: Hamilton; d. 1855 age 70 yrs.; bur. at Poolville; Claim #68238: $38.00 by exec.
Love, Levi	Maj. in 2nd (Lt?) Horse Artillery in 1814; wife, Rebecca d. 25 Feb. 1824 age 50 yrs; bur. at Madison Lake.
Loveland, Andrew	Res: Lenox; Pvt. in 129th Regt.
Low, Peter A.	Res.: Sullivan; Ensign in the 129th Regt.; Claim #2058: $58.00.
Lownsberry, James	Res.: Fenner; d. 1 Oct. 1868 age 86 yrs.; bur. Fenner; Claim #10704: $16.50.
Luther, Andrew	Res.: Sullivan; Claim #26: $44.00.
McDonald, John	Res: Cazenovia. Claim #1711: $58.00.
McElwain, Alexander	Lt. in the 129th Regt.; wife, Rhoda d. 15 Mar. 1809 aged 33, bur. Georgetown. (The date of death is indeed questionable as it is some years prior to the War of 1812. ed.)
McElwain, James	Lt. 129th Regt.; owned Lot #126 in DeRuyter; settled in 1807.
McIntyre, Price B.	143rd Regt.; d. 12 Apr. 1862 aged 85 yrs.; bur. Leonardsville.
McLure, Orin	Served in 3rd Art.
Main, Paul B.	Res.: Brookfield. 143rd Regt.

Manchester, Jacob	Res. given as Madison Co.. Claim #860: $39.00.
Marriam, Elisha	8th Cavalry.
Martin, Darius	Res: Madison; Claim #858: $79.00; d. 15 Nov 1868 aged 76 yrs.; bur. Madison Lake.
Mason, Aaron	Pvt. in a corps of Riflemen.
Mather, Elijah	Res.: Cazenovia; Pvt. in the 65th Regt.; d. 1819.
Mattison, Nathan	Res.: Smithfield. Pvt. 65th Regt.
Maxon, Jeremiah	Res.: Brookfield; 143rd Regt.
Maxon, Joshua, Jr.	Res.: Brookfield; 143rd Regt.
Maxwell, George	Res: Eaton; 1771-1855; bur. Morrisville.
Maynard, Amos	Res.: Madison; d. 27 May 1853 aged 77 yrs.; Capt. in 65th Regt.
Mead, Dr. Sisemus	[Onesemus] Res: Nelson; Surgeon; 1779-1852.
Metcalf, Elijah	Officer in the 3rd Artillery.
Miles, Alanson	Res: Eaton; d. 10 June 1863 aged 87 yrs.; Claim # 5959: $45.50 and #10692: $44.00.
Millard, Clark	Res.: Bolivar. Claim #7872 - $11.00
Miller, Christopher	Res.: Lenox; Pvt. in Beecher's Co. at Sacketts Harbor; Claim #9620: $42.00; Moved to Genesee Co., MI.
Miller, Elijah B.	Res: Brookfield; 143rd Regt.
Miller, John	Res: Lincoln; 1778-1864: bur. Wampsville; Pvt. in Beecher's Co. at Sacketts Harbor.

Miller, Joseph	Res: Brookfield; Pensioned at $96.00 per anum, 21 June 1820: Artillery; 1794-1875.
Miller, Leonard	Res.: Lenox. Claim #23: $53.00 & #10702: $47.00.
Miller, Richard	Res: Canastota; wife, Anna d. 6 Feb. 1860 aged 76 yrs.; bur at Whitelaw: Claim #7540: $11.50
Mills, Levi	Res: Eaton; Pvt. in Bicknell's Corps of Rifleman.
Miner, Nathan	Res: Eaton; Pvt. in 65th Regt.
Mize, Capt. Edmond	Bur. in Madison beside his wife - no stone for him.
Monroe, William	Res.: Sullivan; settled prior to 1796; Claim #4904: $57.00.
Moon, Philip	Res.: Clockville; Pvt. in Beecher's Co. at Sacketts Harbor; wife, Catherine Kern (1790- 1846) bur. at Merrillsville; He moved to Paw Paw, MI. Claim #13431: $55.00 by his son.
Moore, Elisha	Res.: Brookfield; Lt. in 143rd Regt.
Moore, James	Res: Cazenovia; d. 1816. Capt. in the 65th Regt.
More, John	Bur. at DeRuyter - no dates on stone.
Morey, Gideon	1792-1873, bur. at Earlville.
Morgan, Henry	Lt. in the 8th Cavalry.
Mott, John C.	Res: Clockville; Capt. in 74th Regt.; d. 22 May 1839 age 54 yrs.; later lived in Stockbridge.
Morris, Darius	Pvt. in a corps of Rifleman; Postmaster at Eaton in 1832.

Morris, Isaac	Res.: Oneida; 1781-1856; Claim #878: $77.00
Morris, Joshua	Res.: Brookfield; 143rd Regt.
Morris, Zodac	Lt. in 143rd Regt.
Morse, Joseph	Lt. in 65th Regt; wife, Zida d. 14 Feb. 1815 age 32 yrs.; lived Fenner.
Moyer, Daniel	Res: Sullivan; Capt. in 74th Regt.; d. 11 April 1858 aged 32 yrs; bur. Merrillsville.
Munger, Horace	Res: Fenner; Capt. in 129th Regt.
Munger, James	Res.: Fenner; Pvt. 129th Regt; Claim # 7337: $58.00; Moved to Bloomfield, NY.
Munson, Rueben	Res: Lenox; Pvt. in Beecher's Co. at Sacketts Harbor.
Murdock, Ariel	Capt. in 65th Regt.; d. 12 Sept 1826 age 44 yrs.; bur: Hubbardsville.
Murdock, John	Pvt. in 129th Regt; d. 4 June 1840 age 75 yrs; bur. Cazenovia.
Myers, Frederick	Res: Smithfield; 1780-1860; 129th Regt.; Claim #14007: ($13.00) by widow in Cook Co., IL.
Nash, Asa	Res.: Eaton; d. 14 Feb 1815, age 51 (or 55); bur. at Pratt's [Hollow?]; Claim #852 by widow; $43.00.
Nash, Jasper	Res: Clockville; 1793-1854; Pvt. in Beecher's Co. at Sacketts Harbor.
Nash, Thomas	Res: Hamilton; d. 1842 age 53 yrs.
Nash, Willard	Res: Hamilton; Pvt. in 3rd Artillery; b. MA 1796; d. 1873.

Nash, Zenas	56th Regt.; wife Lois d. 24 Oct 1832 age 58 yrs; bur Hamilton Center.
Needham, John	Res: Fenner; Comm. Officer in 129th Regt.; Claim #16314: $50.00; d. 1852.
Nellis, Barnhardt	[Barent] Res: Lenox; 3rd Artillery; Moved to New Bremen, NY. Claim #14787; $55.00.
Nellis, John D.	Res: Clockville; Corps in Beecher's Co; d. Ashtabula, OH in 1849.
Nemiers, John C.	Res: Lenox; Pvt. in Beecher's Co. at Sacketts Harbor; Claim #6592: $58.00.
Newman, Robert	Res: Smithfield; Claim #12758: $60.00.
Nichols, Samuel, Jr.	Res: Fenner; Claim #3261; $47.00 and 10700-$47.00; 1779-1871.
Nichols, William	His wife d. 1 Mar. 1826; she was buried in Perryville.
Niles, Harvey	Res.: Lebanon; Pvt. in a Corps of Rifleman.
Niles, Luther	Res: Lebanon; d. 31 Aug 1876: bur. in Lebanon; Claim #1567: $39.00.
Northrup, Barzillian	Res.: Peterboro; d. 1821 aged 43 yrs.
Olds, Ira M.	Chaplain in 74th Regt.; Congregational minister at Chittenango and Quality Hill.
Osmer, Rev. ___	Chaplain in the 65th Regt.; d. 1814.
Osborn, Phillip	Res.: Lenox; Corp. in Beecher's Co. at Sacketts Harbor; Claim #9839: $38.50; removed to Adams Co., WI.
Ostrander, Henry	Res: Clockville; Pvt in 74th

Ostrander - continued	Regt.; Claim # 2317: $58.00; (1795-1876).
Othroudt, John	Res: Sullivan; Pvt. in Beecher's Co. at Sacketts Harbor.
Owen, August H.	(Alexander?) Pvt. in the 74th Regt.
Page, Daniel	Res: Fenner. Claim # 22: $31.00; perhaps same as that Daniel Page, a tavern keeper in DeRuyter in 1795.
Page, William	Res: Stockbridge; b. VT, settled in 1796; d. 15 Feb 1757 aged 64 yrs.
Palmelee (Parmalee), Charles	- Res.: Sullivan; Lt. in 129th Regt; d. 12 Jan 1843 aged 55 yrs.; bur. Cazenovia.
Palmer, Asher H.	Res: Lincoln; served in 74th Regt.; Claim #14981: $46.00; b. 1794; moved to Rome, NY and d. there.
Palmer, Benjamin	Claim # 7895: $44.00; b. 1795; physician in Oneida, NY.
Palmer, Joel	Res.: Sherburne; Claim #912: $50.00
Palmer, John	Res: Eaton; Claim #14737: $55.00
Palmer, Leonard	Res: Lincoln; Claim #1314: $60.00; removed to Rushford, WI.
Palmer, Noyes	Res: Brookfield; Major in the 8th Cavalry; Claim # 6842: $55.00; Moved to Harmony, NY.
Palmer, Russell	Res: Lincoln; Claim #7774: $50.00 by exec.; Removed to Washtenaw Co, MI.
Palmer, Stephen	Res.: Madison Co. Claim #13820 by executor: $38.00; b. 1771; removed to MI.
Palmer, Stephen W.	1793-1879; Claim #5556: $33.00; Removed to Napoleon, MI.

Palmer, Warren	Res: Brookfield; Pvt. in 143rd Regt.
Parlen, Charles	Lt.
Parker, Joel	Res: Stockbridge; Claim #13790: $11.00; claim made by admins.; d. Georgetown.
Parker, Leonard C.	Claim #859: $60.00; d. 28 June -- age 81 yrs.; bur. Madison Lake.
Parkill, Reuben	Res: Clockville; 1783-1869; Sgt. in Beecher's Co. at Sacketts Harbor; Claim #2315: $65.00.
Parmelee, Jesse, Jr.	Res.: Brookfield; served in the 8th cavalry.
Parson, Daniel B.	Pvt. in a corps of Rifleman; wife, Virtue d. 20 June 1814 age 24 yrs; bur at Madison Lake.
Parsons, Festus	Res: Fenner; Ensign in the 129th Regt.
Pattison, Robert K.	Claim #7083 by administrator, $41.00; d. 29 Sept. 1831 aged 47 yrs.; bur. at Randallsville.
Payne, John C.	Served in 129th Regt; settled in Georgetown in 1804.
Pease, William	Res: Clockville; Pvt. in Beecher's Co. Claim #10202: $20.00. [Was he the William, Jr. who lived in Pompey, Onon. Co. at one time?]
Peck, Talcot	(Pick) Pvt. in Beechers Co. at Sacketts Harbor.
Peebles, William	Res: Sullivan; Claim #2302: $45.00.
Perkins, Cephas	d. 9 Feb 1827, age 52 yrs.; bur. Madison Lake.
Perkins, Elmander	b. MA. 1792-1854; settled in Cazenovia 1803; d. at Lyons, NY.

Petrie, Daniel	Res: Peterboro; Commanding Officer in the Artillery.
Petrie, Jacob	Res: DeRuyter; Claim #2477: $51.00; d. 11 June 1863 age 85 yrs.
Petrie, John H.	Res: Lenox; Claim #879: $51.00.
Phelps, Bradley	(Phillips?) Res: Nelson; Claim #866: $43.00.
Phelps, Isaac	Res.: Lenox. Capt. in the 74th Regt.
Thomas W.	Res: Quality Hill; Lt. Col.in the 74th Regt; d. 5 Sept 1838 age 66 yrs.
Phinney, Zenos	56th Regt.; Cazenovia tavern-keeper.
Pickle, George	Res: CLockville; Pvt. in Beecher's Co. at Sacketts Harbor; 1784-1846.
Pickle, Henry	Res: Clockville; Pvt. in Beecher's Co.; d. Barre (Barry?), MI. Claim #6847 - $55.00.
Pierce, Benjamin	Lt. in 3rd Art; d. 7 June 1817 age 56 yrs; bur. Hamilton.
Pierce, Chandler	d. 2 March 1883; bur. Randallsville.
Pierson, Benjamin	In 129th Regt; settled in Cazenovia in 1793.
Pierson, Oliver	Res: Cazenovia; served in 129th Regt.
Pike, Jesse K.	Aide to a Maj. Gen.; settled in Cazenovia 1798.
Poole, Isaac	Res: Hamilton; in 65th Regt. Wife Margaret d. 18 July 1813 age 25, bur. in Earlville.
Pope, Arnold	Res.: Hamilton; Claim #2101: $62.00.

Popple, Billings	Res: Brookfield; served in 143rd Regt.
Porter, Asahel	Corp. in CT Militia in 1814; d. Sullivan 23 Oct 1830; wife, Margaret.
Porter, Russell	Lt.; d. 7 Apr 1853 age 68 yrs; bur Hamilton Center.
Post, Daniel	Res: Cazenovia; Claim #16795: $60.00.
Potter, John	Res: Stockbridge; b. 1794; settled in 1825; served in New England.
Potter, Stephen M.	Res: Cazenovia; Claim #2172: $25.00.
Powell, Robert	Lt. in 65th Regt; Owned William Parkhurst farm in Lincoln in 1812.
Pratt, Daniel	Res: Fenner (1779-1864); Surgeon in 129th Regt.
Prentiss, Manessah	Ensign in the 129th Regt; d. Cazenovia 1815.
Prosser, William H.	Res.: Madison Co. Claim #9629: $75.00.
Prout, John H.	Claim #8894 by Adminstrator, $60.00; d. 13 Sept 1852 age 76 yrs; bur in Lenox on Lewis Point Rd. [Record lists this man as John G., a res. of Cairo, Greene Co., NY. I doubt it is the same person. ed.]
Putnam, Aaron	Res: Fenner; Claim #5956; $41.50.
Randall, Asa	Res: Lincoln; Pvt. 74th Regt; 1779-1820: bur. Chaffee Cem.
Randall, Elisha, Jr.	Res: Brookfield; 143rd Regt; 1790-1836.
Randall, Nicholas P.	Served in the 8th Cavalry.

Randall, Robert	Res: Brookfield; 143rd Regt; settled 1792; d. 15 Dec 1859 age 85 yrs.
Randall, Roswell	Res: Lincoln; Lt. in 74th Regt; 1777-1853; d. Brooklin [Macomb Co], MI.]
Randall, William	Res: Lincoln; moved to Columbia, MI about 1835; Claim #7878: $38.50; 1779-1862.
Ransier, John J.	Res: Perryville (Sullivan); Claim #8403: $52.00; d. 4 June 1861 age 81 yrs.
Ransom, Elisha	Pvt. in Beecher's Co. at Sacketts Harbor; Claim #1099: $38.50; Moved to Mooers, Clinton Co., NY
Ransom, Russell	Res.: Fenner. Claim #1394: $46.00 and #16790 - $47.00
Ratnour, George	Res: Lincoln; served in 74th Regt.; b. 1795.
Rawson, Jerias	Res.: Augusta, Madison Co. [Oneida Co.] Claim #868: $52.00
Ray, Gershom	Res: Perryville; d. 27 Feb 1857; age 70 yrs.
Raymonds, Asa	Served in corps of Rifleman; merchant in Peterboro.
Rector, John	Res: Bridgeport; d. 30 May 1869 age 85 yrs.
Reed, Stephen	Res: DeRuyter; Claim #755: $35.00 and #756 - $77.00.
Reed, William	Res: Oneida Vally; served in New England; 1786-1852; had son, Edmond.
Reynolds, Zadock	Res: Brookfield; served with 143rd Regt.
Rhodes, James B.	Res: Hamilton; Claim #8819: $21.00.

Rice, Asa H.	Res: Sullivan; Claim #16793 by widow - $22.00.
Rice, Halsey	Res: Cazenovia; served with the 129th Regt.
Rice, Moses	Res: Smithfield; d. of Camp Fever in Lenox 1814.
Rice, Paul	Res: Fenner; Lt. in the 129th Regt.
Rich, Warren	Res.: Hamilton; Claim #1521; $57.00.
Richardson, Asa	Res.: Nelson; Claim #5961: $41.50.
Richardson, Eri	Res: Nelson; Capt. in a corps of Rifleman; d. 7 Aug 1844 age 65 yrs.
Richardson, Joseph W.	Capt in 3rd Artillery; moved to Macomb Co., MI; Claim #8742: $58.00.
Rider, James	Res: Madison Co; claim #14594: $55.00.
Rider, Zenas	Ensign in the 129th Regt; b. 1 Dec. 1785, d. 17 Aug 1858; bur. in DeRuyter.
Roberts, Alvory	Res: Fenner; 1790-1849.
Roberts, John	On Pension Roll in 1840 census of Fenner age 53 yrs. living in Canastota in 1883; drew pension of $8.00 per month.
Rogers, James	Res: Cazenovia; Claim #25: $54.00.
Rogers, John	Res: Brookfield; 143rd Regt; Claim #4681: $54.00; d. 15 Nov 1862 age 82 yrs; bur. Leonardsville.
Root, Thomas	Res.: Cazenovia; Claim #1398: $32.00; d. 15 Sept. 1863 age 85 yrs.

Rouse, Elijah	Res: Lincoln; Pvt. in Beechers Co. Claim #6595; $73.00; b. 1794 d. 1865; bur. at Merrillsville.
Rowe, Samuel	Served in 65th Regt; b. 1762; settled in Madison in 1794.
Saunders, Augustus	Served in 143rd Regt; d. 3 Mar 1868 age 78 yrs; bur. Beaver Creek, town of Brookfield.
Saunders, William B.	Res.: Brookfield; Claim #2743: $38.00.
Savage, John	Res: Cazenovia; Claim #1401: $47.00; wife, Amy d. 1818 age 26 yrs., bur. in Hubbardsville.
Savage, Roswell	Res: Cazenovia; served with the 129th Regt.
Savage, Seth	Res: Cazenovia; Claim #1395: $47.00.
Schuyler, Barnett	(Barney?) Res: Sullivan; Pvt. in 74th Regt.
Schuyler, John P.	Res: Sullivan; Comm. Officer in 74th Regt.
Scott, Amos	Res: Brookfield; Pvt. in 143rd Regt.
Scott, Chester	Res: Brookfield; Lt. in 143rd Regt; Claim #7181: $58.50; moved to Phelps, Ontario Co., NY.
Scott, Jason	Res: Eaton; wife bur. at Poolville. Claim #5965: $88.00.
Scouten, Moses	Res: Cazenova; Claim #2173; $82.00.
Scovil, Lemuel	(Luther?). Res: Cazenovia; Lt in Corps of Rifleman; Claim #7541 by administrator, $100.00. Detroit, MI.
Seeley, John	Res: Cazenovia village 1811; later Sullivan; Claim #8401 by executrix; $21.00

Sexton, Dyer	Lt. in 65th Regt; d. 17 Sept 1862 age 78 yrs; bur. DeRuyter.
Shanland, Thomas J.	Served in the 8th Cavalry.
Shattuck, Justus	Res: Hamilton; d. 28 Dec 1831 age 52 yrs; bur. Hubbardsville.
Shaver, John W.	Settled in Clockville 1811 - later in Sullivan; Claim #17: $69.00.
Shaver, William	Res: Sullivan; Claim #18: $30.00.
Shed, Jonathan	Res: DeRuyter; Lt. in 8th Cavalry; d. 1852.
Sheldon, Samuel	Served in the 8th Cavalry.
Sherman, Richard	Res: Nelson (Fenner?). Claim #5970: $41.50 & #10697: $47.00.
Sherwin, Joshua	74th Regt; Lenox tavernkeeper.
Shipley, Daniel	Res: Clockville and later Sullivan where he d.; served in the 16th U. S. Rifles; pensioned in 1833.
Sholes, Parley	Res: Hamilton; Claim #2103: $58.00 & #2104: $33.00.
Simons, William G.	d. 25 Dec 1854 age 65 yrs; bur. Randallsville
Sims, Joseph	Capt. 8th Cavalry; d 12 Jan 1864 age 90 yrs; bur. Nelson.
Sizer, Asa B.	Res: Lenox; Comm. Officer in U. S. Army.
Sizer, Samuel, Jr.	Res.: Hamilton; served in 3rd Artillery. .
Skiff, Charles	Res: Madison; Comm. Officer in 65th Regt.
Skinner, Isaac	d. 10 Jan 1873 age 77 yrs; bur. Poolville; Claim #1518: $40.00.
Smith, Calvin	Res: Sullivan; Quarter-master

Smith – continued	in 74th Regt; Claim #14464: $13.00; moved to Alleganie Co. [sic].
Smith, David D.	65th Regt; d. 1833 age 50 yrs; bur. Hamilton Center.
Smith, Elijah	Res: Cazenovia; Claim #1400: $46.00.
Smith, Jonathon	Claim #16069 by exec; $50.00; Cazenovia tavern-keeper.
Smith, Luther	129th Regt; d. 1862 age 78 yrs; bur Nelson.
Smith, Peter S.	Res: Peterboro; 65th Regt.; 1795-1857.
Smith, Peter H.	Res.: Stockbridge. Claim #870 - $29.00.
Smith, Rueben	Res: Perryville; d. 3 May 1856 age 86 yrs.
Smith, Warren	Res.: Brookfield; served with 143rd Regt.
Snell, John J.	Res: Chittenango; Claim #13175 by widow, $70.00.
Snow, Barnabas	Res: Smithfield; Comm. Officer; Claim #10976: $28.50; moved to Oak Grove, WI.
Snow, Isaiah	Comm. Officer in 65th Regt.
Snow, Sewell	Quarter-Master with the 65th Regt.
Snyder, Adam R.	74th Regt; Claim #6596: $73.00; 1789-1846.
Snyder, Martin	Res: Lincoln; 74th Regt; Claim #869; $64.00.
Southworth, William	(Southport ?) Pvt. in 143rd Regt; Lt. in 1815.
Sowter, A. Isaac	Res: Canastota; Claim #5083: $55.00.

Spaulding, Hiram   Pvt. in Beecher's Co. at Sacketts Harbor.

Spencer, Ichabod   Res: Quality Hill; Quartermaster 74th Regt.; d. 7 Jan 1857 age 72 yrs.

Spencer, J. Austin   Res: Lenox; Sgt. in Art; b. 1790 - d. 1857 at Utica, NY.

Spencer, Jonathan   Ensign.

Spencer, Oliver   Cornet; Claim #5105 by Admns., $55.00; Moved to Midddleburg, NY.

Spencer, William   Capt. in Reg. U.S. Army in War of 1812. Postmaster and tavernkeeper at Wampsville

Spinner, Jonathan   Comm. Officer

Squires, Orrin   Res: Hamilton; Claim #1520; $57.00

Stacy, Nathaniel   Chaplain 65th Regt. Settled in Hamilton 1797

Stanley, John F.   Res: Cazenovia; On pension roll 1883 at $8.00 per month.

Stanley, Joseph H.   Res: Cazenovia; Claim #1403; $46.00.

Staples, Elijah   Res: Poolville; d. 22 March 1878 age 84 yrs.

Starr, Elisha   Res: Cazenovia; Capt in 129th Regt.

Stebbins, Charles   Res: Cazenovia; served on staff of Gen. Hurd; 1789-1873

Stebbins, Gaius   Res: Lebanon; Lt. in 65th Regt; Claim #7863: $38.50; moved to Sparta, Kent Co., MI.

Stebbins, Isaac   Drummer; served in NY Militia; pensioned at $96 per year 7 Nov 1814; d. 3 June 1821; Claim #14446: $70.00; family moved to Avon IL.

Stewart, Charles	Res: Stockbridge; Claim #877: $62.00; d. 14 June 1856 age 73 yrs; bur. in Eaton.
Stewart, Ezra J.	Res: Stockbridge; Claim #863: $40.00; d. 1866 age 73 yrs.
Stewart, William	Res: Eaton; Claim #13865 by widow, $100.00
Stocking, Roderick	Pvt. in Beechers Co. at Sacketts Harbor.
Stone, David	Comm. Officer in Bicknell's Brig; Claim #5966: $28.95; d. 5 June 1863 age 76 yrs; bur. Erieville.
Stowell, Enoch, Jr.	Res: Nelson; d. 3 June 1859 age 92 yrs; Also served in the Revolutionary War.
Summers, Charles	Res.: Madison Co. Claim #1386: $58.00.
Sweet, Jonathan	Res: Nelson; Claim #864: $55.00; d. 1 Apr 1865 aged 73 yrs; bur. at West Nelson.
Sweeting, Lewis	Res: Sullivan; Claim #1110: $66.00; Served from Saratoga Co.; b. 1793.
Sweetland, Zadock	Res: Cazenovia; Quarter-master in 129th Regt; d. 1865 aged 73 yrs.
Tabor, Joseph	Res: Lenox; Claim #14982: $140.00. May be same as Joseph of Lincklaen, Chenango Co. who made claim #6943: $65.00.
Taggart, William	d. 12 Nov. 1847 aged 77 yrs; bur. Lebanon.
Taylor, Asa	Res: Lenox; 74th Regt.; d. 13 Sept 1829.
Taylor, Jonah	Res: Brookfield; Capt. in 143rd Regt; d. 13 Jan 1837 age 65 yrs; bur. Unadilla Forks [Chenango Co., NY.].

Taylor, Myton W.	(Myron?) d. Smithfield; merchant in Peterboro; son Edwin W. Taylor.
Taylor, Nathan	Served in 65th Regt; b. 1789; a hatter in Madison.
Taylor, Rueben	Res: Georgetown; Claim #856: $60.00.
Taylor, Thomas	Res: Fenner; Claim # 10714: $47.00 and #1561: $41.00.
Teneyck, Jacob	Res: Cazenovia; Capt in 8th Cavalry; settled in 1807; d. in Georgia 1853.
Thomas, Samuel	Comm. Officer in 129th Regt; d. 12 Mar. 1861 age 81 yrs; bur. Cazenovia.
Thompkins, William B.	Res: Lebanon; 65th Regt; d. 15 Mar. 1862 age 81 yrs.
Thompson, Calvin	Res: Eaton; Claim #5958: $38.00; 1778-1866.
Thompson, Rufus	Res: Lincoln. Sgt. in 129th Regt. at Sacketts Harbor. Built sawmill at Alene; [Came from] Union, CT. Also a veteran of the Revolution.
Thorington, Wallis	Pvt. in Beecher's Co at Sacketts Harbor.
Thurston, Daniel	Res: Stockbridge.
Tidd, Ebenezer G.	Res: Eaton; Claim #5963: $63.00; d. 29 Sept age 77 yrs.; bur. at Morrisville.
Tiffany, William E.	Res: Stockbridge; Claim #865: $63.00.
Tift, Royal	Res: Cazenovia; Cornet in 129th Regt.
Tillinghast, Daniel	Res: Morrisville; d. 22 Aug 1827 age 59 yrs.

Tompkins, Brownell	Res.: Madison. Claim #952: $41.00; d. 4 Oct. 1864 age 78 yrs; bur. Madison Center.
Torphy, John	Res: Nelson; wife, Polly d. 5 Aug. 1850 age 67 yrs., bur. near the Welch Church [in Nelson].
Torrey, Lyman	d. 29 Aug 1822 ae 67 yrs.; bur. in Earlville.
Tryon, Zebina	d. 19 Aug. 1829 age 45 yrs; bur. at Whitelaw.
Tucker, Samuel G.	Res: Madison; Claim #1381: $39.00; wife bur. at Madison Lake.
Tuckerman, Jacob, Sr	Res: Eaton; moved to Clinton, NY.
Turner, Benjamin	Res: Cazenovia and Nelson; Claim #71125: $21.00; Supervisor town of Nelson.
Turner, John	Res: Nelson; served in Batt. of Riflemen; Claim #14734: $55.00; moved to Ashtabula, OH.
Tuttle, Abraham	Res: Clockville; Corp. in Beecher's Co.; Claim #8840: $56.00 by executrix.
Tuttle, Isaac	Res: Lincoln and Eaton; Claim #17223: $50.00 by administrix.; widow and son bur. at Pratt's (Hollow?).(This man applied from Peekskill, NY - may not be same. ed.)
Twogood, Joseph	Res.: Fenner. Claim #10703: $47.00; merchant at Chittenago Falls also #24: $50.00. (Name for claim in rolls is spelled Turgood, but certainly the same man. ed.)
Tygert, David	Res: Stockbridge; Claim #6848: $38.00

Tyler, Roswell	Res: Hamilton; served in 65th Regt.
Ufford, Joel	Res: Lenox; d. 12 June 1848 ae 75 yrs; bur. on Lewis Point Rd.
Underwood, Marvel	Res: Cazenovia; 129th Regt; d. 23 Oct 1835 ae 60 yrs; son, Marcus.
Van Acker, Henry	Pvt. in Beechers Co. at Sacketts Harbor.
Van Alstine, Abraham	Res: Sullivan; Claim #6332; $58.00; moved to Wayne Co., NY.
Van Alstine, Andrew	Paymaster 74th Regt.; d. 30 Aug 1839 ae 55 yrs; bur. at Wampsville.
Van Alstine, John B.	Pvt. in Beecher's Co.
Van Alstine, John J.	Res: Sullivan; Claim #15354 by widow, $95.00; moved to Plymouth, WI. (MI?)
Van Alstine, John, Jr.	Pvt. in Beecher's Co.
Van Alstine, John M.	Pvt. in Beecher's Co.
Van Duesen, Jeremiah	Res: Clockville; Pvt. in Beecher's Co. Claim #6594: $50.00; 1795-1863
Van Vetchen, Barent	(Barney?)- Served in 74th Regt.
Vedder, John H.	Res: Clockville; Claim #875: $44.00.
Wagoner, John C.	Res: Lebanon; 65th Regt; 1797-1878; bur. at Morrisville.
Waldron, Cornelius	Res: Sullivan; served in 74th Regt.; Claim #59: $47.50 moved to Cicero, Onondaga Co., NY.
Walker, David	(or Daniel S.) Res: Lebanon; 56th Regt; Claim #7669: $20.00; moved to Newbury, OH.
Walrod, Peter	Res: Clockville; 74th Regt.; 1775-1849.

Walters, Oliver	d. 10 Feb. 1814 age 34 yrs; bur. Earlville.
Walton, Ward	Res: Quality Hill; served with 74th Regt.
Ward, Peter	Res: Stockbridge; Claim #6849; $38.00.
Ward, Richard	Res: Eaton; served in 65th Regt.
Ward, Samuel	65th Regt.; d. 22 Sept. 1816 ae 35 yrs.; bur. Madison Lake.
Warmuth, Conrad	Res: Fenner; Claim #10698: $47.00.
Warner, Seth	Res: Lenox; Pvt. in Beecher's Co.; Claim #10684: $38.50. moved to Van Buren, Onondaga Co., NY.
Warren, Chester	Ensign in the 74th Regt.
Wattros, Joseph	Res: Nelson; Ensign in the 65th Regt; Claim #10850: $80.00; moved to Owego, Tioga Co., NY.
Webb, Henry B.	Res: Madison; Claim #6863; $55.00 and #12370: $60.00.
Wells, Barker	Res: Erieville; d. 30 Jan. 1857 ae 80 yrs.
Westcott, Oliver	Res: Eaton; Claim #854: $43.00; d. 26 Mar. 1876 ae 77 yrs; bur. Erieville.
Wetherby, David	Res: Hamilton; Claim #3818: $19.00.
Whaley, John H.	Res: Georgetown; Claim #5972: $36.00 and #6494: $30.50.
Whipple, William	Res: Georgetown. Claim #2804: $38.00
White, Clark	Res: Brookfield; served with 143rd Regt.
White, Luther	Claim #8069 by widow, $41.30; d. 3 May 1828 ae 49 yrs.

Whitford, Warren	Pvt. in 143rd Regt.
Whiting, Thomas	Cornet.
Whitman, Henry	Pvt. in 74th Regt.; Lenox Constable 1815-1817.
Whitney, Ebenezer	Res: Nelson; served in the 129th Regt; d. 1 July 1856 ae 85 yrs.
Whitney, Thomas	Ensign in 129th Regt.
Wickwire, Garret	Res: Hamilton; served with the 65th Regt.
Wilber, Jeremiah	Res: Hamilton; Claim #1384: $39.00; also lived in Fenner.
Williams, Elijah	Res: Georgetown; d. 1856 ae 70 yrs; bur. at Morrisville. There was also a man of the same name who applied from Manlius #1196 & #4684 - recd. $16.50 & $50.00.
Williams, John	Res: Cazenovia; 129th Regt; d. 14 July 1853 ae 63 yrs.
Williams, Joseph	Res: Cazenovia; 129th Regt.; Claim #12732 by admns, at Cicero, Onondaga Co., $17.00; d. 1856 ae 88 yrs.
Williams, Robert	Served with the 8th Cavalry.
Williams, Warren	Res: Brookfield; Claim #3036; $30.00; d. 27 Aug. 1862 ae 72 yrs.
Wilson, Ebenezer	Served with the 8th Cavalry.
Wimple, John V.	[Wemple] Res: Wampsville and Lenox; Pvt. in Beecher's Co.
Winchell, John	Res: Cazenovia; died from exposure in War of 1812.
Wood, John K.	65th Regt; d. 3 Oct. 1866 ae 85 yrs; bur. at Madison Lake.
Woodhull, Stephen	Res: Madison; Claim #1522: $19.00.

Woodworth, John	Res: Lenox; in Beecher's Co; Claim #10933 by admns, $65.00; d. in Steuben Co. [NY]. (Didn't find. ed.)
Woolever, John, Jr.	Pvt. in Beecher's Co.
Wormuth	See also Warmuth
Wormuth, Conrad.	Res. Fenner. Claim #5416: $55.00
Yale, John	(or Joel?) - Pvt. in Beecher's Co; d. 21 July 1837 ae 57 yrs; bur. at Quality Hill.
Yates, John B.	Res: Chittenango; Capt. in Artillery; 1784-1836
Yorton, John N.	Pvt. in Beecher's Co; 1790-1859; bur in Central Square, NY; Claim #670; $67.00.
Yorton, Paul N.	Res.: Sullivan. Claim #13819: $50.00.
Young, John	Res: Sullivan; Claim #1404: $6.00; d. 11 July 1869 ae 74 yrs; bur. Gates Cemetery.
Young, Truman	Res: Cazenovia; Ensign in the 129th Regt.
Youmans, William	Res: Eaton; 1781-1853.
Prentice, Ensign M.	Res: Cazenovia, d. at Sacketts Harbor, 17 Nov. 1814; left wife and seven small children. (Caz. Pilot, Nov. 1814.) Possible veteran. See Meyer p. 190.
Thomas, Abraham	"Old Mr." Thomas aged 93 yrs., a veteran of the War of 1812, will apply for his pension. (DeRuyter Gleaner 29 Jan. 1879). Died Thurs. last, age 90 yrs., a veteran of the War of 1812; has resided with his dau., Mrs. Noble Babcock for the last few years. DG 4 March 1880. Meyer, p. 234

BIBLIOGRAPY OF MADISON COUNTY, NEW YORK
GENEALOGICAL SOURCE RECORDS

Biographical Review: The Leading Citizens of Madison County, New York. Boston, 1894. 706 pp.

Ellsworth, Anzolette D. and Richmond, Mary E. New Woodstock and Vicinity, past and Present. (1901) Repr. Pipe Creek Publications, Inc., Finksburg, MD, 1993. 172 pp.

Houck, Clara Metcalf et al. Vital Statistics From Chittenenago, New York Newspapers, 1831-1854. (1970) Repr. Mt. Airy, MD, Pipe Creek Publications, 1994. 154 pp.

Meyer, Mary K. and Scott, Joyce Clark. Cemetery inscriptions of Madison Co., NY, Vol. 1. (Towns of Fenner & Nelson). Severna Park, MD, 1961. 88 pp.

Meyer, Mary K., ed. Abstracts from Madison County, NY Newspapers in the Cazenovia, NY Public Library. Mt. Airy, MD, Pipe Creek Publications, Inc., 1991. 336 pp.

Scott, Joyce Clark. Madison/Morrisville Observer. Deaths & Marriages. n.d.,n.p. 199 pp.

Smith, Gertrude. Deaths, Births, and Marriages from Newspapers Published in Hamilton, Madison Co., NY. Mt. Airy, MD, Pipe Creek Publications, 1991.

Smith, James H. History of Madison and Chenango Counties, NY. Syracuse, 1880. 760, xxi pp.

www.ingramcontent.com/pod-product-compliance
Lightning Source LLC
Chambersburg PA
CBHW061259040426
42444CB00010B/2423